Download
Worksh

My goal is to help you accomplish as much as possible with this book and that's why I've created additional worksheets, guides, and resources to help you implement what you learn. This book is packed with strategies and tools, which are great to learn about, but I want you to take action on them.

Download your worksheets, guides and additional resources and keep them handy as you read the book. You can download them at www.evolveyourweddingbusiness.com/ book.

Clone Your Best Clients

How to Take the Guesswork out of Your Marketing and Attract More Ideal Clients

Heidi Thompson

Evolve Your Wedding Business Publications
San Diego

Dedication

To my amazing husband, Joe, for supporting, encouraging and believing in me even when I don't believe in myself. I love and appreciate you with all of my heart.

Contents

Introduction

If you've ever said, "I don't know how to reach my potential clients. I know they're out there, I know they exist, I know other people are working with them, but I don't know how to reach them."

Or if you've ever said or thought, "I'm doing all these marketing tactics that I've heard about, but not attracting any clients."

Or if you're thinking, "I'm attracting clients, but they complain about prices, they're total bridezillas; they're nightmares, they want everything for nothing."

I get it, and you're not alone. In fact, the vast majority of wedding professionals that I work with come to me with these exact problems.

Throughout this book, you're going to learn how to attract your ideal client, not just any client, because you can do better than that. You don't have to just take the scraps that get thrown your way. You don't have to deal with having clients that don't value what you do, continually question prices and expect your services and expertise for next to nothing.

You're about to learn how to use the Clone More Clients System to identify the clients you love to work with and create a marketing plan unique to your business that consistently attracts more of your ideal clients.

Are you ready to start attracting your ideal client without the constant struggle?

Let's do this!

1

Why Your Marketing Isn't Working

Before we can move forward with changing your marketing, we have to look at what you're doing now and why it isn't working.

You've been doing all of the things you've heard work for getting more clients. You've built a website. You're spending time on Facebook and Instagram and Pinterest. You're paying for advertising, wedding fairs, WeddingWire, The Knot and you're attending networking events.

So why isn't your marketing bringing you clients?

I find this is best explained through a thought experiment so imagine this: You're tasked with building the house of your dreams. There's no budget too big but you have to build it alone. You're probably starting to think about how you're going to create this absolutely perfect and stunning home with luxuries like a massive pool and, of course, a hot tub to relax in. You'll build a huge, beautiful kitchen like the ones you see on HGTV and a gorgeous outdoor space for you and your family and friends to enjoy. It'll surely put the most beautiful mansions in the world to shame.

You're excited, so you hurry to round up your tools to get to work. You have every tool you'll need from hammers and nails to power tools. You've got this, and in your mind, you're fantasizing about a house that looks a little something like this.

You work and work and work on your soon-to-be glorious new home with all of the tools you have.

You step back to marvel at your creation, and in reality, it looks more like this.

What the hell went wrong?! You had every tool

at your disposal and no budgetary restrictions so why didn't this come together the way you thought it would?

Because you didn't have a blueprint.

All of the tools in the world won't do you any good if you don't have a blueprint. Without it, you're just hammering pieces of wood together that won't line up in the end because you didn't start with the end in mind.

Marketing is no different. Attracting clients doesn't happen just by doing the recommended marketing tactics.

Yes, marketing tactics are important, but they are nowhere near as important as having a plan, and not just any old plan. Just like any old blueprint won't get you the house you want, any old plan won't get your business to where you want it to be. You need a plan centered around who you want to attract, and that will help you determine which marketing tactics and strategies to use.

This book isn't just about creating that plan; it's about not having to make it up and hope that it works. I'm not a big fan of hope-based marketing; especially when you can find out exactly what should be in your plan directly from the people who you're trying to attract. You don't have to come up with this plan out of thin air.

I'm going to show you exactly how to mine your ideal clients for the information you need to create the perfect plan to attract them. The best part is, they're going to tell you a lot of this themselves.

I find that about 90% of the problems that wedding professionals come to me with are a result of not having a plan specifically tailored to their ideal client. The root of your frustration, confusion, and overwhelm come from not having an understanding of who your ideal client is beyond their demographics like age range, income level and location, and how to attract them. Yes, you may know they're a woman who is 25-40 who lives in or near New York City, but that doesn't tell you what to do to attract them. We can do better than that.

When you get this right, you'll be like Marie Burns Holzer, a wedding officiant in Southern California who got crystal clear on who her ideal client was and went from working with extreme budget brides who didn't value what she does, to attracting and easily booking her ideal clients who don't balk and her prices and are excited to work with her. Some of them have even changed their wedding date so that Marie could perform their ceremony!

Sounds pretty amazing, right?

Since the person you're marketing to is going to drive your marketing decisions, we need to define exactly who that person is.

2

Why Having an Ideal Client Doesn't Limit You

I want to ask you a question: Who are you marketing to? You can't just market for the sake of it, that's like doing archery without having a target—you're not going to do so well because you're not going to know where to aim. You're not even going to know how you're doing because you have to know how close to the target you're getting. You're just going to be a crazy person spinning around firing arrows at will.

Your ideal client is the target, and understanding them will ensure you are aiming in the right direction. That understanding is the foundation of your business, and it has a direct impact on how successful your business is.

I want you to think about who it is that you're marketing to. How would you describe them? I must point out that trying to appeal to everyone will kill your business. Not even massive corporations can appeal to everyone. They don't have the budget or the bandwidth, and even if they did, it's logically impossible.

Now, I know what you might be thinking: "But I can help anyone who needs my help!" You may feel like you should market to everyone and anyone with a pulse and a credit card, and that makes sense if you're trying to reach the maximum amount of human beings. The problem is, you don't have the money to market to everyone, and even if you did, you're not for everyone. Even Apple, the most profitable company in the world, has its haters.

It may seem counter-intuitive, but your marketing should focus only on the people who are most likely work with you. You can't be a perfect fit for everyone, and by trying to do so, you're flushing your marketing budget and your time down the toilet. When you narrow your focus, you will save money and effort while you attract better clients.

Still not sold on the idea of narrowing your focus?

If you had a heart attack, would you rather see a cardiologist or a general practitioner? And would you rather see a random local cardiologist or one who has a lot of experience with patients who have had heart attacks like the one you had? Cardiologists aren't for everyone, but they are in demand by patients who fit their target market and tend to be paid significantly more than general practitioners are.

The reason most people would choose to go to the cardiologist is that they're specialists and they provide a specific service for a specific group of people. As a result of narrowing their focus, specialists get paid more for their work. Cardiologists in the U.S. can earn $300,000 – $400,000 on average compared to the $189,000 base salary that a family practitioner earns. Cardiologists that specialize even further into a subspecialty and bring in $500,000 per year. Specialists don't see as wide an array of clients because they are very, very focused. But because they are very focused, they become the go-to person for their ideal client.

You can't be everything to everyone; you have to focus.

I promise you this will make your life a lot easier.

TAKING YOUR IDEAL CLIENT FROM AN AMORPHOUS BLOB TO REAL LIFE

A lot of people have a fluid idea of a nonexistent, amorphous client, they kinda sorta know who they maybe want to work with. But it's vital to have an exact target, not only because it helps them find you, but because it helps you find them.

If you're shooting a bow and arrow, and you don't know where the target is, chances are you're not going to hit the target. But if you know where the target is, it suddenly becomes so much easier to hit it. That's what happens when you hone in on who your ideal client is, exactly.

Many wedding professionals say: "I know who my ideal client is, it's a fun couple between 20 and 35 who doesn't have time to plan their wedding and can afford to pay my prices."

At face value, it appears this wedding planner has defined and identified her ideal target market and client. It covers the basic attributes—they're fun, they fit within a desired age range, they don't have time so that's the problem they're looking to solve, and they're willing to pay your prices because they value what you do. There's an enormous problem with that, though. People aren't demographics, and there are a lot of different types of people who fall into that "between 20 and 35 years old, doesn't have time, can afford to pay my prices" group.

So, is your 30-year-old a Walmart shopper or would she never be caught dead there?

Is your 30-year-old covered in tattoos and loves artistic, creative things, or is she the total opposite?

As you can see, there are a lot of different types of people in any given demographic, and if you think about the people in your life, you'll see this. There are a lot articles floating around the internet about how Millennials behave or how Baby Boomers behave, and I'm sure when you read these and think: "I'm not like that, my friends aren't like that, we think about that in this other way." You can't lump people together if you want to figure out what they want and care about, so your services can be the answer to their needs and desires. Understanding your ideal clients' needs, and your ability to meet them is the key to marketing that works.

Instead of describing your ideal client as a massive, amorphous group, it makes more sense to describe one member of that group as an actual human being. If they were your friend and you were describing them to another friend, what would be the things that you would say about them? That's likely very different from the demographics most ideal client exercises will point you to.

You wouldn't tell a friend that you met this awesome woman and she's between 20 and 35, and she's very busy. Come on, no one speaks like that! So, we have to get back to reality to narrow down who this person is and what they want.

Does your ideal client value tradition? Is that important to them? Or are they in love with everything that they see on Offbeat Bride?

Understanding what your ideal client values, likes and dislikes is far more valuable to your marketing plan than demographic based traits. Why? Because our personalities and values directly impact our consumer behavior.

If you take yourself, for example, I'm sure there are certain places you love to shop, and there are places you can't stand and that make you feel gross. You hate the customer service, and their products are inferior. These preferences are based on your values.

If, for example, you value being green and environmentally conscious, and you're the type of person who takes their own shopping bags to the grocery store that you walk (or bike, but never drive) to, and you try not to waste if at all possible, then, the chances of you buying something, especially something disposable, from a big box store like Walmart, are probably pretty slim.

You're far more likely to shop at a grocery store that shares your values. Maybe you shop there because they have an eco-friendly distribution system and have free trade and recycled goods.

Chances are, you're going to choose Whole Foods over Walmart. Whole Foods stands for something, and whether a brand says they stand for something or they don't say it out loud, you can tell what they're all about. So, consider what values you have that drive your purchasing decisions.

GETTING TO KNOW AND UNDERSTAND YOUR IDEAL CLIENT DOESN'T HAVE TO BE LIMITING

I'm often asked if it's possible to target clients with different income levels or if narrowing down your ideal client means you have to choose a specific income range. You absolutely can target clients in multiple income levels by offering different packages at different prices. Chances are, the people you have worked with have something in common, and it's going to be something more personal than their income level—it's going to be that they all value something similar.

Do you have to choose between doing

traditional and contemporary weddings? You could if you want to, but you don't have to. Look for the intersections of what your potential clients have in common and define your ideal client based on them. Yes, some of them have more traditional weddings, and some have more contemporary ones, but at a fundamental level, your ideal clients will probably have some personality traits and values in common.

Our values directly impact our consumer behavior, and of course they do, because where you decide to spend your money is an incredibly emotional and personal decision. You don't want to support a brand that you hate. Your values directly impact your consumer behavior, whether you're shopping for groceries or deciding who you're going to book for your wedding and the same is true for your clients.

3

"Bride" Is Not an Identity

I want you to keep in mind that your ideal client is a whole and multidimensional person. Many of the problems that arise when wedding professionals inaccurately market their businesses come from not having an understanding of who their ideal client is as a whole person. Your ideal client is not just a bride or a groom. He or she is a whole human being with an entire life outside of wedding planning that consists of individual values, hopes, dreams, fears, hobbies, and life experiences. He or she is filling the role of bride or groom at this moment, but ultimately, that is not his or her identity as a person.

We often silo our clients and look at them as just a bride or just a groom, and they're not just that. Until you truly understand who they are as human beings, it's very difficult to market to them effectively. Their role in a wedding isn't who they are as a person, and marketing has to appeal to personal values. There's nothing value-based that comes from just being in the role of a bride or a groom. So instead of thinking of them as just this weird siloed off demographic, I want you to think of them as a whole person, a unique person, as a friend.

Most professionals in the wedding industry are too vague with defining their ideal client, and that's why standard, generic ideal client exercise doesn't work for them. The way they describe their ideal client is broad, and if you are guilty of doing this, it may be because you simply don't yet have the level of detail needed to clearly describe your ideal client— which is okay because that's what this book is going to help you figure out.

I want you to identify exactly who your client is. If there's someone you worked with previously and you'd like to clone them and work with them over and over again, I want you to dig into who they are. If you went out for a beer with them what would you talk about? What would they say? I want you to describe them like you're talking about one of your friends. What do they like to talk about? What do they geek out on? That's the stuff that matters. It sounds trivial, but I promise you that these are the details that will help you effectively define and market to your ideal client.

If you know your ideal client is obsessed with Game of Thrones, you can work that into your marketing, and suddenly you are so much more attractive because they feel like you get them. The goal is to eliminate uncertainty and become specific about who you serve. An effective way to define and become clear on your ideal client is to identify a few actual people and use their combined characteristics to create an ideal client profile. Why can't we just go with the vague ideas we have about this person in our heads? Well, as my father always told me, don't just assume because it makes an ass out of you and me (ass+u+me). Who wants that?

SETTING YOURSELF APART

If you're just another wedding planner or photographer in your city, then couples are going to compare you to everyone else. Now, if you're the go-to photographer for tattoo-loving couples who read Offbeat Bride and give the middle finger to tradition, or the go-to planner for couples who are Americans, often the children of immigrants, and they really value their Hispanic heritage and they want to incorporate that part of their identity into their wedding, you put yourself in your own category.

Suddenly you're not just a photographer or a planner. You're the clear best choice for your ideal client. There's the vanilla that is everyone else, and then there's you.

That doesn't mean you're only allowed to work with your hyper focused ideal client. If a prospective client loves your work and you love them back, even though they aren't 100% on target with who your ideal client is, that's okay! It's your business, and you can make the decision to work with them or not.

For example, I went to a conference called *The Boss Mom Retreat*, and it's one of the best events I've ever been to. I am not a mom, but I love everything the brand, and the founder, Dana Malstaff, stands for. I can relate to the Boss Mom brand and I knew that I wanted to be at that event and I'm so happy that I attended. I may not be Dana's exact ideal client, but if she hadn't positioned herself as the go-to mentor for boss moms, a description I kept hearing from my boss mom friends, I would have never known she existed.

If you're the go-to photographer for tattoo-loving couples who read Offbeat Bride and give the middle finger to tradition but one couple you attract doesn't have any tattoos, you can decide to work with them if you'd like.

Just like if you're the go-to planner for couples who are Americans, often the children of immigrants, that really value their Hispanic heritage and a white girl like me wants to work with you because I'm in love with all things Mexican and I know you're going to fulfill my vision, you can decide to do that.

Setting yourself apart attracts your perfect ideal clients as well as those more fringe but still awesome clients.

So who do you want to be the go-to person for?

When you market your business, you're going to talk to that person, and as a result, you will attract those perfect clients.

Do you see why your ideal client is so important?

All of the marketing in the world can't fix the lack of understanding your ideal client. Who they are and what they value drive *everything* from the words and images you use on your site, to what you post on social media to how you work with them.

YOUR IDEAL CLIENT IS YOUR FOUNDATION

Defining and understanding your ideal client is a critical piece of your marketing strategy. Do not pass go, do not collect $200 if you don't have a deep understanding of your ideal client. Spending marketing dollars and valuable time on specifically targeted marketing strategies focused on your ideal clients is far more efficient and effective than marketing to no one in particular and hoping that something sticks. Hope-based marketing is a waste of your time and your money.

Here's the key—and this is the disconnect that most people don't see—when your marketing isn't aligned with the problem your ideal clients want you to solve, they will not work with you. When I say "problem," we're not curing cancer here, these are not life or death problems, but you are solving a problem or concern that is very real for your ideal client. Maybe the problem is that they are too busy, so the problem that you're solving for them as a wedding planner is that you're swooping in to take over the tasks they simply don't have time for. But maybe that's not the problem, and you are just assuming that it is.

Maybe the real problem is that every wedding your ideal client has ever been to has been boring, unimaginative, and generic and they want theirs to be more unique, and they're also very busy. If you market to them about just being busy, and you miss what they're really concerned about (their wedding not being boring), they're not going work with you because they don't feel like you understand them. In a way, we have to be mind readers, but we don't have to read minds—there's a much easier way.

So, what are you supposed to do? To create and implement targeted marketing that reaches your ideal clients, and solves the problems they have versus the one we imagine they have, you must find out what their problems really are, not just your assumptions about them. When you make these assumptions, it's highly likely that your marketing isn't going to connect with your ideal client because it's based on nothing more than a guess. I am going to show you how to go from making unfounded assumptions about your ideal clients to finding out exactly what problems, values, and desires they have.

4

Investigation Warm-Up

Before we go deep into investigator mode, we're going to do some initial intel-collecting.

THE EMAIL METHOD

Do you have an email list? If you do, the easiest way to get started is to contact your email subscribers. If you don't have an email list, you can engage your previous clients and ask them about what they struggled with or what they wish they would have known. Here is a sample email that you can use to reach out to them:

Hi <name>,

I'm working on some new blog posts, and I want to make sure I can help you in the best way possible. What are you struggling with when <insert the problem that you solve> or what questions do you have about <insert the problem you solve>?

Thanks!

<your name>

The problem you choose to insert might be "planning your wedding" or "choosing your stationery".

Quick Tip: *You can use this email tactic for doing research when you're trying to come up with blog post ideas, deciding what your email opt-in should be, checking in to make sure your marketing is aligned with your ideal clients, and anytime you need to know* *what's going on in the minds of your ideal clients. It's an incredibly useful and versatile tactic!*

If you've ever seen an email from me that asks you to reply and let you know what you're struggling with the most, this is the tactic I am putting into action. I don't want to assume what the problem is because you may be struggling with something I'm not aware of, and I need to ensure that I am offering the right solutions and marketing in a way that lets my ideal clients know that I can help them.

KEEPING TRACK OF RESPONSES

Any time you ask your ideal client what they are struggling with, whether it's via your email list, on a phone call, in person, or on social media, you'll want to record the responses you get word for word. When you take the words that your ideal client uses and then use those words in your marketing and on your website, suddenly your clients can see themselves in what you're saying, and they feel that not only do you get them, but you solve the exact problem they have. Suddenly there's a connection, and it's not you versus every other photographer, you're the one that connects to them, and sets yourself apart.

Keep these responses in a place where you can easily access them like Google Drive, Evernote, or a notebook so when you need to describe what you do and what problem you solve. You can also use your ideal client responses when you need to re-write your 'About Me' page, by going back and using their own words to create marketing that connects with them.

Let me give you an example of how this works. I know a fantastic copywriter who was working for a drug rehab clinic that was struggling to stand out from their competitors. Many drug rehab clinic websites use very clinical terminology, as you might expect, and this client just wasn't getting great results with their website. Before she began optimizing the text and buttons on the website, this copywriter began listening. She looked at Amazon book reviews about drug rehab, and she focused on the 3-star reviews people left because, although those people benefited from the book, it didn't deliver the value expected. She found a quote in one of those reviews that was pure marketing gold: "If you think you might need to go to rehab, you do." This was a direct quote from someone who had been to rehab and was sharing his personal experience. She took that quote and used it on the clinic's website, and their bookings went through the roof because they used normal human language that connected with their ideal client. We don't speak the same languages in our business as the people who buy from us. We use a lot of industry-specific jargon that is common to us but is an entirely different language to those outside the industry. Listening helps to work out the jargon and your natural inclination to add that in, so take your ideal client's exact responses, word for word, and use them.

USING SOCIAL MEDIA

Another great way to gather intel is to run polls. You can run them in Facebook groups where you know that your ideal clients are going to be or on Twitter. If you've ever seen me run a poll in my Facebook group, it's because I'm gathering intel.

You can also ask "What are you struggling with when <insert the problem that you solve> or what questions do you have about <insert the problem you solve>?" in Facebook groups and on your other social media sites. Keep in mind not to get spammy and promotional in this process. This is not about promotion; it's about listening and gathering intel.

LOOK AT YOUR REVIEWS

Remember Marie Burns Holzer from Chapter One? When she was honing in on her ideal client, it occurred to her that she should look to see what the couples she loved working with most said about her in their reviews. Why? Because one of the qualities she knew she wanted in a client was that they would rave about the service she offered.

Marie started going through all of her reviews on Yelp, Facebook, WeddingWire, and The Knot to see what they had in common. A vision became clear. Her couples often don't know what they're doing when it comes to planning their perfect wedding ceremony, but they want a wedding that is personal and fun. They are often spiritual but not religious or are an interfaith couple. Before she knew it, she had three ideal client types that she could use to categorize her favorite couples! Since gaining clarity on who these people are, over 80% of her clients fit into one of these three ideal couple types and, as a result, she is a lot happier in her work.

Identifying her ideal clients was a big change for Marie because, like many wedding professionals, she started with basically anyone who would book her. She now looks back and reflects,

"I remember when you first started talking about your ideal client on an episode of your podcast, and a light bulb just went off! I couldn't believe that I had just been throwing my net hoping to catch anything without realizing how ineffective that was.

It also resonated with me because I was listening to you teach this while I was driving home from a wedding that was the *opposite* of my ideal client. I didn't feel connected to the couple, and while they seemed happy enough with the ceremony, I felt empty when I left their celebration, which is *NOT* how I normally leave a wedding.

I was upset and listening to you tell me that I needed to target my ideal client specifically was revelatory!"

ANALYZE BRANDS YOUR IDEAL CLIENT LOVES

Study the sites that your ideal client loves to see what's popular, what they're writing about, and how they're marketing. If you know that your ideal bride buys 90% of her clothing from Anthropologie, although that's not directly related to weddings, we're looking at her as a whole person, so it most certainly matters. Visit the Anthropologie site and observe how are they talking about the products that they're selling. What makes them so appealing? Suddenly, by playing investigator, you can pull from these other areas of their lives to use in your marketing.

I recently gave a presentation on this topic to a group of wedding professionals, and one of them perked up and said: "I'm so happy you said that because I know that every single bride I work with is a huge Kate Spade fanatic." If you're not familiar, Kate Spade makes high-end handbags and accessories, so suddenly she knew exactly where to look for inspiration on the tone and messaging for her brides.

If you don't know what brands your clients love, ask them. You can also refer to your Audience Insights in the Facebook Ads Manager to see what other pages your fans like.

Get started with your investigation warm-up, and in the next chapter, we're going to dive into how to interview your clients to get the more in-depth intel you need to attract more people just like them.

5

Who to Interview and Getting Them to Agree

We've already established the importance of identifying the problems and values of your current, potential, and previous clients. It is essential to understand your clients to ensure your marketing is aligned with their needs and wants. Aligned and effective marketing also reduces disconnects which can lead to losing clients. A disconnect is what leads to people saying "Eh, no, I don't want to hire you," as opposed to them being so absolutely sold and certain that you are the perfect person for them.

But how do you choose who to interview and get them to agree to do an interview with you? That's what we're going to tackle in this chapter.

First, though, I want to make sure you're in the right mindset before beginning this interview process.

YOUR MINDSET

I encourage you to adopt a curious mindset and be genuinely curious about why people do what they do. That's going to serve you well throughout this interview process.

You've probably heard entrepreneurial quotes about how potential clients may not know what they want, but they know what frustrates them, and it's your job to connect the dots. Your job in these interviews is to uncover frustrations and emotions, and then connect the dots for them.

Henry Ford said that if he had asked people what they wanted, they would have said "A faster horse" because they didn't know a car was a possibility. They didn't know a better solution was available and that wasn't their job. Their job is to tell you the problem. Your job as a business owner is to provide the solution for that problem.

WHO TO INTERVIEW

Before you send out interview invitations, you need to decide who would be best to interview.

I would recommend following this order:

- Group 1. Your clients, people you're either currently or just wrapped up working with.

- Group 2. Your previous clients.

- Group 3. Your wider audience, which includes blog readers, email subscribers, your social media followers, people in relevant Facebook groups, etc.

The reason why the most important interviews

you will conduct will be with clients or past clients is because they have paid you. They decided to work with you, and they're who you want to attract more of, so their opinions are very important and, in these interviews, you can learn a lot about why they chose to work with you.

The goal is to talk to your favorite past clients, the ones you wish you could clone and work with over and over again. You'll be the happiest person in the world if you can work with people like this all of the time. If you had a horrible client, don't interview them because you don't want to attract more people like them.

Within Group 3, your wider audience, you can interview people who you think might fit your ideal client profile. Basing this on a hypothesis at first is okay. Everything we do in business is based on a hypothesis, and then we test it and find out if it is true or false. Your ideal client, like all things in your business, evolves over time. Your ideal client today may not be the ideal client you had two years ago or will have five years from now.

ASKING FOR THE INTERVIEW

Since your clients and previous clients are the priority, you'll email them first. Here's an email template you can use that I've pulled directly from *The Wedding Business Collective*:

Hi <name>,

I have absolutely loved (change this to present tense for current clients) working with you and {name of partner}. If I could work with couples like you all the time, I'd be in heaven!

I would love to have a chat so that I can ask you some questions that will help me find more couples like you and {name of partner}. It'll only take about 30 minutes and I promise it'll be painless. It might even be fun! *(If you want to you can incentivize this by adding in an extra to their package they've already purchased. Just make sure it doesn't cost you a lot of money or time.)*

I've made it super easy for you to choose a

> date and time that works for you, just click here and take your pick!
>
> Speak to you soon!
>
> <your name>

In this email, I've noted why I want to talk to them—because I want more people like them and that's very flattering. People love feeling special, of course, who wouldn't? Then, you're specifically requesting a verbal conversation and not just an email or a survey; you want to ask questions to help you find more people like them.

Another important point is that I assure them it'll only take 30 minutes. Be respectful of people's time. Let them know up front what they're committing to so that they know how much time to set aside. How much does it suck when you go somewhere that's going to take "just 5 minutes," and it takes an hour? If you've ever been to the California DMV, I'm sure you know what I'm talking about.

In the last line, I've made it easy for them to choose a date and time that works best, and provide a link for them to schedule the call. You want to avoid those annoying back and forth emails about whether "this date is good for you." Adding more barriers and hassle make it easier for them to say "No" to your interview request. You are asking them to do you a favor so make it as easy and convenient as possible for them to say "Yes."

If you don't already have a scheduling tool, sign up for a free account with Calendly. You can put specific days and hours you want to make available for interviews and Calendly integrates with Google Calendar, so if you have something already booked on your Google Calendar, it won't allow double booking.

Here's an email template you can use for someone who isn't a client:

Hi <name>

I loved what you said about <X topic> in the <XYZ Facebook group>, and I couldn't agree more.

I run a photography business (give website) and I would love to have a chat so that I can ask you some questions that will help me attract people like you. I'm not trying to sell anything; I'm trying to learn what I can do to find more of my ideal clients and who better to go to than someone I can tell I'd love to work with?

It'll only take about 30 minutes, and I promise it'll be painless. It might even be fun! (If you want to you can incentivize this in some small way.)

I've made it super easy for you to choose a date and time that works for you, just click here and take your pick!

Speak to you soon!

<your name>

The example I've used in the first paragraph is "I love what you said about the X topic in the XYZ

Facebook group, and I couldn't agree more." You are citing a specific conversation and saying that you're in this group together. Even though you don't know each other, you have something in common, and that helps build rapport.

Then you want to get into who you are, for example: "I run a photography business" (or however you describe your business) and give a website, and "I'd like to have a chat so that I can ask you some questions to help me attract more people like you."

This next part is critical. "I'm not trying to sell anything. I'm trying to attract more of my ideal clients, and who better to go to than someone I can tell I'd love to work with." You want to make this absolutely clear because you can see how some people will think you're going to get them onto this free call and then try to sell them something. That's not what you're doing. **Do not try to sell on these calls.**

And like the last email template, you set the expectation that the call will only take 30 minutes, should be fun, and you can incentivize it in some small way if you want. You can offer them a Starbucks gift card or something like that but not a discount on your services because again, you're not selling.

I've also made it easy for the person reading this to use the link to your scheduler, so you don't have to go back and forth deciding on a time.

> **You can download these email templates & interview tips to help you get the most out of this process at www.evolveyourweddingbusiness.com/ book.**

6

Conducting the Interview

I'm going to give you some questions to ask during the interview, but your job is to be an investigator. Think about the way T.V. investigators, inspectors, and detectives handle things when they're doing an investigation. They ask a lot of questions and based on the information they receive, they ask follow-up questions.

Interviewing is about listening and digging for more information. It's easy, especially if you like the people you are interviewing (and you probably do because you want to work with more of them). But, for this interview, you're going to do a lot more listening than you are talking. You're going to ask a question, and then you're going to shut up and listen intently.

I'm going to walk you through an interview technique that is going to help you get great answers out of your clients. It's called the laddering technique, and it's all about digging deeper.

If you're a stationer you'd ask:

"Why did you select those wedding invitations?"

The answer might be something like "I really liked the traditional design and the heavy cardstock."

This gives you the attributes that they like heavy cardstock and traditional design, but it doesn't give you the reason why. There are underlying reasons and motivations for everything, and purchasing decisions are no different, so we want to dig into 'why.'

To take the laddering technique to the next rung of the ladder you ask:

"Why is the heavy cardstock important to you?"

Your interviewee says: "Oh you know, heavy cardstock makes the event seem and feel more formal, substantial, and important."

This answer gives you insight about the person's relationship to the attribute. It tells you what they associate with the attribute, so heavy cardstock = formal, substantial and important. But we're not going to stop here because this isn't where the gold is.

To take the laddering technique to the next rung, you then ask:

"Why is it important that your wedding is more formal and substantial?"

And they might say: "Well, my friends all had

fabulous weddings and I really want to do something on par with them."

Ding ding ding!!!

Now you understand their core value, the motivation for the decision based on the actual reason for the decision. This is a "keeping up with the Joneses" motivation. It's lying under the surface, and you wouldn't have known unless you conducted an interview in which you were digging deeper.

So, when somebody gives you an answer in an interview, it isn't enough to just leave it there. If they tell you they really like the traditional wedding invitations, ask why. Why is that important? What does that mean to them?

These are the questions you want to ask to dig deeper on each level. I use this interview process anytime I start to feel a little bit fuzzy or disconnected from the people that I want to attract. This interviewing technique gives me the clarity I need to ensure I am effectively marketing and speaking to my ideal client.

YOUR TECH SETUP

I highly suggest you record the interviews so you can refer to them, or listen to them and use the exact words the interviewee used. Let the person you're interviewing know you're recording, and why (so you can refer to it, and you can't write that fast) and ask them if that's okay with them. Most people aren't going to have a problem with it.

Quick tip from a podcaster: when you are recording, you can see the time count in minutes and seconds. When the person you're interviewing says something you want to come back to, write down the time. It will help you get through it so much easier. If you know that at 12 minutes and 14 seconds there's something you want to go back to and

> *get the exact words from, it's easier if you*
> *make a note of it.*

I use Skype to run of all my calls. It's free, and you can use a call recorder app like Ecamm Call Recorder for Mac or Pamela for PC.

If you'd prefer to use your phone, you can use Automatic Call Recorder for Android or ipadio or Google Voice for iPhone.

If you want a written copy of your recording, you can find someone on Fiverr to transcribe the calls for you at a very reasonable rate.

QUESTIONS TO ASK DURING THE INTERVIEW

You have identified and scheduled the people you want to interview, now, you need to decide what questions to ask. In this section, I will help you find the perfect questions to ask each person you interview.

A lot of people get hung up on the demographics of their ideal client, and yes, it's important to know that she's a female between the ages of 25 and 35 who lives in London, but there are a lot of females between 25 and 35 who live in London. To know and understand who your client is and how to find more just like them, it is imperative to go beyond the demographic questions—to go below the surface to who they are at their core.

What you want to find out about them are the things that make them who they are, the things that someone would use to describe them if they were fixing them up on a date with you, or the things they would say if describing a friend to you. They don't say, "she's 25 to 35 years old and lives in London." Below are sample questions you can use in your interviews. You can take your pick, just make sure you are asking the question and then digging deeper with follow-up questions.

QUESTIONS TO ASK EVERYONE

- What brands do you love? *(Maybe they reply that they're an Apple fanatic. You should then ask what they love about Apple products to uncover the emotional connection to the brand.)*

- Do you read wedding blogs? Which ones?

- Do you read wedding magazines? Which ones?

- What is your favorite social network to spend time on, and why? What do you love about it? On the flip side, what social networks do you hate and avoid?

- When it comes to finding potential wedding vendors, where do you look?

- What method of communication do you use most often? *(This will help you learn more about how to best communicate, or how to think about communication with your ideal client. For example, if you know they don't answer their phone, that's going to change the way you do things.)*

- What do you do in your spare time?

- We all geek out on something, what do you geek out about?

- How would your best friend or your partner describe you? *(This is an especially good one because it requires people to step outside their normal frame of reference for themselves.)*

QUESTIONS TO ONLY ASK CURRENT AND PAST CLIENTS

- How did you find me?

- What hesitations did you have about working with me? *(Dig deeper here finding out why that made them take pause and hesitate to choose you.)*

- What made you choose to work with me instead of another X? *(They might say, because you do this, then you then ask why this is important to them.)*

- What do you look for in the wedding

professionals you work with? Why does that matter to you? *(This is definitely going to be a ladder question, where you get a more face value answer, and dig deeper and find out more and more and more.)*

- What has been the biggest challenge in deciding on stationery for your wedding, or finding the right stationer <insert what you do>?

- What has been frustrating to you in the process of planning your wedding? *(Ask this question even if you aren't a wedding planner, because you're going to learn a lot about the frustrations that are directly adjacent to what you offer, and you can help them with this through your contacts on your site.)*

- Why did you decide to go with whatever product or service they purchased? *(Dig deeper)*

- If you were recommending me to a friend, what would you say? *(This is another one that requires them to step out of their frame of reference and think about what they would say to someone else. This question has been awesome for me. I've learned a lot of what people valued about working with me that I had taken for granted. It definitely changed the way I present and market myself.)*

Conducting market research via interviews is an invaluable tool for identifying, finding and staying on track with your ideal clients. I recommend conducting a cycle of interviews at least once per year. It is worth the effort and your business will see a return on that investment.

> **You can download these interview questions along with a list of all of the tools mentioned in this chapter www.evolveyourweddingbusiness.com/book.**

7

Crafting Your Message after the Interview

Now that you've conducted your interviews, you can craft your message and marketing based on what you've learned. Add the exact words your interviewees used—**do not paraphrase them**—to a document or a tool like Evernote. This document will be your copy bank. Copy, simply defined, is the words that you use to sell things—the words on your website, the words that you use to describe your packages and pricing, and the words you use on social media or in an ad. By creating a copy bank with the exact words that your ideal clients use, you will never be stuck and unable to describe what you do, or why your ideal client should choose to work with you. The copy bank will be there for you. You'll have exact words from clients and potential clients, and when you echo those needs and wants back to them, they will trust that you understand them, because you do. You listened!

Use a spreadsheet to input the answers to the questions you asked so you can see commonalities and patterns. Personally, I love taking notes by hand, but patterns are a little more difficult to see that way, so if you put them in a spreadsheet it makes it easier to search and see what those patterns are.

Psychology is the basis of effective marketing, and the insights you gather will help you understand more about why people say and do the things that they say and do. So, what are the core values that you've uncovered? What motivations do your interviewees have in common?

As you review your recordings, reflect on the assumptions you had going into the interview that were either proven right or proven wrong. What do you need to change about how you approach your marketing? Maybe you focus on one particular facet of what you do, or how you do it but it turns out that isn't why people hire you.

Maybe you think that having handmade invitations is a priority to your clients because they inherently value someone taking their time to put those together. It might be true that they value handmade invitations, but they might value them for an entirely different reason. They might value them because it makes them look better than their friends. Don't be surprised if you come across insights that you didn't expect. We all make assumptions, but when we dig deeper into our clients' motivations behind their actions and words, we can offer services that better meet their needs.

CRAFTING YOUR MESSAGE

Looking back at what you learned from the interviews you conducted, how do the interviewees talk about you and what you did for them? Yes, you planned a wedding, or you created their stationery, or you took their photos, but beyond that, how did you add lasting value?

In order to craft marketing messages that appeal to your ideal client, you must focus on the benefits instead of just talking about the features.

A feature is a distinctive attribute or aspect of something—that something is your product or service. For wedding planners, this includes hours a client gets with you, checklists, budgets, vendor recommendations, etc. For photographers, it's the album you deliver, the number of hours you're at the wedding, how many prints the client gets, etc.

Features are how most wedding professionals present what they do, but they aren't what matter to the client most, so they don't sell as effectively as benefits do.

A benefit is an advantage or profit gained from something. How do the features of your products or services benefit your clients? Maybe you save them time, money, or stress. Maybe you make it possible for the couple to revisit and share their wedding day memories for generations. The benefit is much more emotional and by listening to the way your clients talk about what you did for them and how you made them feel you can more accurately present your benefits.

Benefits sell for you because we make purchasing decisions emotionally, and then we justify them rationally. As much as we'd like to think we're rational beings that make choices rationally, it's simply not true.

Your client doesn't know what it means when you say "8 hours of coverage." As a photographer, this is what you do, but it's not what matters to them. But, if instead of saying "8 hours of coverage," you say, "I'll be there to capture the fun you have with your bridesmaids as you get ready, and all the way through the reception so that when your dad busts out his goofy 70's dance moves, I won't miss a moment. You'll have priceless photos of that day to look back on for the rest of your life."

Doesn't that sound much more compelling?

One of those descriptions is cold, factual and unexciting. The other is emotional, and your client can imagine what it will feel like and how important that benefit is to them.

So look back at what people told you in your interviews. What benefits are they describing? Those are the things that matter most to them.

When you find someone describing a benefit, don't edit it. Use their exact words. Your clients have a perspective on what it is like to work with you that you can't have because you're too close to your business. They are telling you exactly what words to use to attract more people like them. You don't have to guess anymore. How awesome is that?!

A CATEGORY OF ONE

As you review what you learned in your interviews, think about what your clients (or potential clients) said about you and how that sounds different from how others in your industry describe themselves. This is a huge opportunity for you to set yourself apart from your competitors and put yourself in a category of one.

If you're thinking, "But how can I be in a category of one? I plan weddings, and other people plan weddings too," consider this: If you don't differentiate yourself from your competitors, the only choice potential clients have is to compare you based on price. That makes you a commodity, and it's the exact opposite of what you want.

Let me ask you this: What brand of sugar do you buy? Do you fill up your car at the closest gas station or do you seek out a particular brand? When you moved into your home, did you choose your utility providers based on price comparison?

All of these—sugar, gas, utilities— are commodities. It's easy to compare them based on price because there is no real differentiating factor. If you are not emphasizing why someone should hire you over a competitor, and you don't understand the value (that's where the benefits come in) you deliver to your clients and what they care about, you're allowing yourself to become a commodity. They don't know what else to ask you because you haven't built a connection or demonstrated your value to them.

Humans compare things; it's in our nature. When all people have to compare is price, the person who is undercutting you will always win. You have to give them something more than price to make their decision. You have to demonstrate that you understand them by marketing to their values and showing them how you can help them get what they value. (Hint:

What they want is not you, you are simply a vehicle to help them get what they want.)

Nobody buys things because of what they represent at face value. They buy things because of the result they will get. Have you ever gone to the store and thought, "I'll buy this floor cleaner because I really like floor cleaners!"? I hope not because if you do, you have bigger issues than your marketing.

People buy cleaning products so that they can have a clean house and you can go even deeper into why someone wants a clean house. When I lived in the UK, there was a commercial for a toilet cleaner that insisted that your guests are judging you based on how clean your toilet is. I thought it was weird because I would hope my friends aren't that shallow, but I couldn't deny that it was brilliant because it spoke to people who want to impress their house guests.

Many companies tried to sell MP3 players in the late '90s before Apple created the iPod. The reason those companies failed is because they sold it as a 2 GB MP3 Player which meant nothing to anyone. The same thing applies to how you describe what you offer.

Apple took a different approach and sold the iPod as "1000 songs in your pocket." Overnight, the iPod took off because people understood what it did for them. They put themselves in a category of one. Sure, other people sold MP3 players, but Apple wasn't selling MP3 players; they were selling "1000 songs in your pocket" so you don't have to lug around a CD case.

In your interviews, you learned what clients value, and now it's time to put those insights to work.

BE THE YODA

Star Wars is not about Yoda; it's about Luke Skywalker's journey. But Luke's journey wouldn't have happened if it weren't for Yoda. You are not the hero in your client's journey. You are the Yoda to their Luke. Your job is to show them what is possible and help them achieve their desired results.

That's why, if you want it to be effective, your marketing can't be all about you.

Does your website (or your social media posts) read like this? "I studied for years, and I won this award, and I shoot weddings in this particular style so book me now because I'm soooo awesome"? If your website contains lots of personal pronouns like us, me, we, I, and our, then you're trying to be Luke when you should really be acting like Yoda.

Your content needs to pass the "So what?" test. When you write, put yourself in your client's position and question every sentence with "So what?"

A wedding planner might say, "We recommend vendors to our clients" . . . **So what?**

So they don't have to find them without our guidance . . . **So what?**

So they know their wedding will be in good hands . . . **So what?**

So they can enjoy their engagement without feeling stressed or worried about who to trust.

They don't care about what you do, dear Yoda. They care about what you help them do. Make use of the word "you" and tell your audience what they will get from working with you. Speak to them, not at them.

This simple mindset shift and better understanding of human behavior will help you so much with your marketing. Remember: Make it about them, not you.

WHO IS IT FOR?

Once you nail down the benefits of what you offer, it's time to review your ideal client interviews to find the common threads that tie these people together.

What did you learn from your interviews about

who your ideal client is as a person? Look back at the answers you go to these questions, and you'll start to see your ideal client in a more personal light:

- "What brands do you love?"

- "What do you do in your spare time?"

- "We all geek out on something, what do you geek out about?"

- "How would your best friend or your partner describe you?"

These are all questions that focus on who this person is outside of their role of the bride or the groom, and it's important that you learn about them in this way so that you can attract them and speak their language.

If you've interviewed past clients, you likely know what their personality is like to some extent. Make a note of that as well. Are they always the one to make light of a situation? Are they laid back? How would you describe them based on your interactions with them?

Putting all of this information together is going to help you figure out how and where to market to your ideal clients and how to communicate with them. For example, if they're all casual, fun-loving people, it doesn't make sense to communicate in a corporate tone to them. It makes a lot more sense to put some wit into your marketing to reflect that casual, fun tone that will resonate with them.

PUTTING IT TOGETHER

You've uncovered who your ideal client is as a human being (and not just a bride or a groom), what they care about, and what results you deliver that they value. Now it's time to put that all together into your simple elevator pitch.

A simple elevator pitch says who you work with and what you help them with, in the simplest, distilled down way possible.

Esme Krahn is a wedding planner and a member of *The Wedding Business Collective*, and it's easy to see from her website (www.bodamaestra.com)

that she helps Latin-American couples who want to honor and display their family roots on their wedding day create a memorable and culturally authentic wedding experience.

That description clearly sets Esme apart from the other wedding planners in the Washington D.C. area because she's not *just* a wedding planner; she's the go-to person for this group of people and delivers a unique result.

When people ask me what I do, I say: "I help amazingly creative wedding professionals grow their businesses without going crazy in the process."

Your simple elevator pitch is the foundation of your message. You can easily expand on it and go more in depth using what you've learned about them as people to turn it into your 'About Me' page.

Below, I have included content from my 'About Me' page, where I've simply taken what I do and added in more benefits and emotion and used "you" so that my ideal client can identify themselves as one of these people:

> "If you were paid based on your talent alone, you'd be swimming around in a Scrooge McDuck-ian style vault right now. You're an uber creative wedding professional that is killing it on the creative front.
>
> The only problem is you want to book more clients and grow your business and even though you're doing all the things you hear will help, it's not working for you.
>
> You bust your ass to wow your clients and grow your business. Hard work is no issue for you. But you're wearing all the hats in your business from CEO to customer service to doing the work your clients hired you for, and the non-stop grind of doing it all by yourself is wearing on you.
>
> You're READY to take your business to that next level and maybe even quit your day job.
>
> But you just don't know how to make that a reality. You feel stuck.
>
> Believe me; I get it! And you're definitely not alone.
>
> Running a wedding business doesn't have to be difficult and painful. I'm here to help you."

The next time someone asks what you do, use

your simple, but well-crafted, elevator pitch. Use it at networking events, bridal shows, and in your social media bios. Expand it and use it on the 'About Me' page of your website. Knowing who your ideal clients are and what results you deliver for them makes the rest of your marketing so much simpler because it gives you something to build on and to check in with if you're not sure about how you're marketing yourself.

Now that you know what to say to attract your ideal client, it's time to choose where you're going to do that.

8

Choose Your Channels

One of the most common things I hear wedding professionals say is, "I'm too busy" or "There's just too much to do."

There is no shortage of things you can do to promote your business, but you don't have to do everything. Not everything matters. You just need to choose the best ways to reach your ideal client and focus on those. The 80/20 rule tells us that 80% of our results come from 20% of our efforts. Focus on that 20%.

Before you go any further, look back at your

interview responses and list the ways that your ideal clients found you, where they searched (specific blogs, WeddingWire, The Knot) and what social media platforms they love and use.

This is where you're going to focus. There's no use spending time on Snapchat if your ideal clients aren't using it. An exception is if you use a specific platform for another strategic purpose like connecting with other wedding professionals or journalists. And if you want to test something new, but keep in mind that it's a test and you may not get the desired results.

Start by reducing the amount of time you spend in places that your ideal client doesn't pay attention to. That may mean that the WeddingWire account you're paying for and hoping will work isn't worth renewing because your ideal clients don't use WeddingWire and you're not getting bookings from it.

There are many ways to market your business, so I'm going to break them down by where they fit within your sales funnel.

YOUR SALES FUNNEL = DATING

What would you do if a stranger came up to you and asked you to marry them?

Unless you're itching to marry a stranger, you'd probably be kind of freaked out, uncomfortable and would look for a way to escape the situation, right? You probably don't realize it, but this is exactly what you're doing to your potential clients when you expect them to land on your website and get in touch with you to have a sales conversation.

There is a process that we all know and understand when it comes to meeting someone, getting to know them, dating them and then getting more serious with them and it doesn't just happen overnight.

The sales process is no different. That is why you need a game plan for taking these potential clients from total strangers to totally in love with you, and that plan is called a sales funnel. Your potential clients move through the sales funnel step by step, date by date, getting to know and love you and closer to being ready to work with you.

> You can download the sales funnel worksheets to help you map out the stages of your own sales funnel at www.evolveyourweddingbusiness.com/book

WHEN YOU FIRST LOCK EYES

There are many different ways to attract clients, and it's something wedding professionals ask me about a lot. Keep in mind, you don't have to do it all, you just have to do what works for you.

Advertising

Advertising is one of the first things that comes to mind when most wedding professionals think about how they're going to get themselves out there, but there are some important things to consider before you pull the trigger.

1. Is your ideal client active where you're advertising?
2. Advertising doesn't come first; it comes last.

Marketing (and that includes advertising) without a strategy is a recipe for disaster.

The point of advertising is often misunderstood. Yes, it's to generate leads for you but how does it fit into the other parts of the marketing mix?

Think of it this way. Marketing is the engine in your car. Sure, you can have a nice-looking car without an engine, but it's not going anywhere. The same applies to your business.

Advertising, on the other hand, is the sassy flame paint job on the side of the car to draw attention to it. But here's the thing, if you have flames painted on a car with no engine, it's still not going anywhere.

Your advertising can supercharge your

marketing efforts, but it is not a replacement for them. You can't be all flames and no engine if you want to get anywhere.

So, what are you supposed to do?

Well, there's an order to these things. First, you put the engine in the car, and *then* you paint on those sick flames. Not the other way around.

That means that first, you develop your sales funnel, the way you capture leads from your website and nurture them, and then you paint flames all over that bad boy.

You need a clear path for people to take from landing on your website to becoming a client, and the first step is getting them onto your email list. From there your email marketing will nurture them and educate them and move them along the sales process. If you have consultations in your business, that would be the next step and then make the sale.

That is what you have to have in place before

paying to send a bunch of people to a website that doesn't generate leads for you.

What good are website visitors if they just land on your website and then leave?

As you're trying to map this out in your head, work backward. It's easier to reverse engineer the process than the other way around. For example, you want to make a sale. What comes immediately before that, and that, and that? Unless you can answer that question all the way back to someone landing on your website, it isn't the right time for you to spend a bunch of money on advertising. Spending money on advertising should not be a gamble. Instead, you should have a sales funnel, so you know that the money you're spending on advertising takes people down a predictable path to becoming a client.

Advertising shouldn't be about paying and praying; there is a strategy to advertising. Once you have a sales funnel and know how people move through it, the math to figure out your return on investment is surprisingly simple.

Inside *The Wedding Business Collective*, there is a course on 'Selling With Email Marketing' where I take members through the entire process of setting up this lead generation system and calculating the math that helps you make advertising decisions. Here's a snapshot of that:

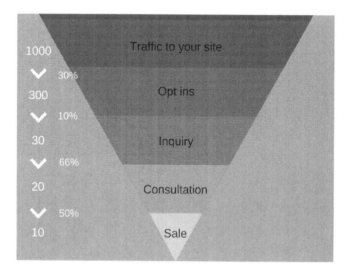

1000	Traffic to your site
∨ 30%	
300	Opt ins
∨ 10%	
30	Inquiry
∨ 66%	
20	Consultation
∨ 50%	
10	Sale

At the top, you start with 1,000 people coming to your site, and 300 of them opt into your email list and so on down the line until the sale. There are some exciting things about doing this math (which is more than I can say for most math).

You can make a significant impact by making relatively small changes. If you know that 50% of the people that you have a consultation with convert into paying clients, you can work on your sales skills to boost that percentage.

If you charge $1,000 per client and you get ten clients for every 1,000 visitors, you know you can spend no more than (and hopefully a lot less than) $10,000 to acquire those clients without going into the red.

Now, obviously, that leaves you no room for profit or payment for your work but let's say you know you need to make $900 net revenue on each of those $1,000 clients to pay yourself and cover expenses. Well, then it's pretty easy to see that you can afford to pay $100 to acquire one client.

Now you know how much you can afford to spend on advertising. Woohoo!

Using this math allows you to look at your current and future advertising spend to see if it's working for you. If you find yourself paying more than you can afford, then it's time to try something new. If you're paying $1,000 and you're getting ten clients out of it, awesome! If you're getting 20 clients, even better! If not, then you know that you need to make some changes.

And yes, that means digging in and changing things in your advertising and lead generation strategy, but wouldn't you rather know that the numbers aren't working so that you can do something about it?

If you're doing the pay and pray method of advertising where you just kind of hope it all works out for you, you're not going to know how many leads it takes to book one client, and how many leads you need to generate from an ad to make it worthwhile. You won't know if an advertising opportunity is working well for you or not and you may very well keep spending money on it because you're afraid to pull the plug.

Being armed with a strategy allows you to make advertising work for you by turning those website visitors into leads and then clients. It also allows you to identify when it's not working, and it will empower you to pull the plug when it's not worth your money because you'll be able to see it in black and white and not have to rely solely on how you feel about it.

If you're busy painting those sick flames on your car with no engine, stop. It's time to do some engine work. Don't worry, though, we're going to dig into every piece of your sales funnel so that when you do advertise, you get results.

Based on what you learned from your interviews, where would be the best places to advertise to reach your ideal clients?

Social Media

Social media sits at the top of the funnel because it's a great way to bring people into your funnel, but it's not so great at selling, which is what a lot of people try to use it for. When you try to sell on social media, you're proposing marriage before the first date. Social media is best used to help you secure the first date with a potential client.

Many people think that social media is a magic pill that's going to transform your business and make you rich overnight. It's not. It's a tool, and like any other tool, your results are going to depend on how you use it.

I use social media to drive people to my blog posts & podcasts, get them to sign up for my email list and learn about my followers through conversation and listening. Because I use social media in a way that leads people down the road to eventually working with me, I get results from it and you can too.

Many wedding professionals have forgotten that

social media is meant to be, you know, social. Instead, they use it as some sort of megaphone tied to the roof of their car Blues Brothers style and just shout promotional messages *at* their followers. Social media is not about you, and talking at people is not going to be effective. Social media is about making genuine connections and building relationships with people.

Based on what you're currently sharing on social media – would you follow you? Why should anyone follow you? A big part of marketing is putting yourself in your potential client's shoes, so what would make them want to follow you? You are an expert so make sure you're delivering value in your social media posts by giving them a tip or some inspiration, which includes sharing your blog posts.

Consistency is one of the most important ingredients in effective marketing and when you go dark on your social media accounts then randomly pop back up it conveys that you are not professional or dependable. It looks like you don't take your business seriously and can make a potential client wonder if you can't keep up with your business tasks, how can you be trusted with their wedding?

I get it; you're busy! That's why I'm a big fan of using tools that help save time like MeetEdgar, Buffer, Hootsuite and SmarterQueue. You don't have to do it manually, and you don't have to be on social media all the time to be consistent!

Yes, Facebook reach is down, and while that sucks, we all got a good free ride for a while. Now, you either need to run Facebook ads or earn your reach by getting your fans to engage with you. Your Facebook reach is not likely going to make or break your business, and if it is, that's even more of a reason to build an email list as I teach in *The Wedding Business Collective*.

The same goes for the number of followers you have on social media. The point of social media is not to collect as many followers as possible—it's not Pokémon. Instead, focus on engaging with people and sharing valuable content, especially when it's on your blog because then your social media drives traffic to your site. That's win-win!

And keep in mind that just because you've shared a blog post or another piece of valuable content once doesn't mean that you can't share it again. In fact, you should share it again because not everyone saw it and tools like MeetEdgar and SmarterQueue can automate that for you. Reusing and recycling isn't just good for the environment; it's good for your sanity and your marketing.

> **Based on what you learned from your interviews, which social media platforms are your ideal clients using?**

Blog

You've probably heard that you should blog, but do you know why?

I get it; you have a lot to do, so why add blogging to your never-ending to-do list? There are some very good reasons to not just blog but to make it a priority.

Google loves you for it

More blog posts mean that your site will have more pages indexed with Google which helps your SEO (Search Engine Optimization). When you create new content, Google comes back to your website more often, and that helps your search rankings. Google loves fresh content, in fact, you are penalized for not creating new content. If you want more people to find you via Google search, blogging is the way to go.

It gives your social media a real job

Many wedding professionals use their social media profiles to tell people to book them and not much else. That's why those people don't get results from social media. Your blog posts give you something helpful to share on social media to get people to come to your website.

You can easily break up a top 10 tips blog post into ten separate tweets that link back to your post. That drives traffic back to your site where they can learn more about you, what you do and how you can help them.

It brings people to your site

I hate to break it to you, but no one is going to come to your site to excitedly read your services page over and over again. It's just not how we use the internet.

However, when you have interesting and helpful blog posts, your website visitors will spend time on your site reading them. This means that they will learn more about you and what you have to offer. It also gives them a reason to come back which is critical for wedding professionals because couples spend a lot of time researching before making a decision to meet with someone. When your website has nothing to offer, they aren't going to remember you.

When you position yourself as a helpful resource

instead of just a service provider, you become much more valuable to your potential clients, and they remember you. Your website visitors may not be ready to book you yet, but by giving them a reason to come back, they remember you when it is time to buy.

Making decisions about who to hire for a wedding is a big deal and can be daunting to a newly engaged couple, so they need time to research and figure out what they want. Couples do a TON of research before booking someone and providing them with content reminds them who you are and how awesome you are.

Not sure what to write about? I've got you covered! I've got 37 blog post ideas waiting for you, and you can download those and all of the other worksheets for this book at www.evolveyourweddingbusiness.com/book.

Based on what you learned about your

> **ideal client during your interviews, what will you blog about?**

THE FIRST DATE

Your potential client has made it to your website, and it's time to propose the first date. Sales is like dating, and asking someone to get married before the first date would be weird, but nevertheless, most wedding professionals ignore this and try it anyway.

The problem with that is that you are proposing something that is completely out of sync with the trust you've earned. That's why you don't marry a stranger, and that's why you don't hire a stranger.

What path are visitors expected to take when they land on your site?

Most people haven't thought about this, but it

can be the difference between someone getting in contact with you or just leaving your site.

Most wedding professionals give the following options to their visitors:

- About

- Services

- Photos/Portfolio

- Blog

- Contact

When someone visits your website while they are researching their options, they will most likely view these pages and then leave because they aren't ready to contact you for a sales conversation and that is the only option you're giving them. People just don't get married on the first date.

In a world of comparison shopping, how can you ensure that more of your website visitors actually get in touch with you?

First, stop and think about why they are visiting your site to begin with. Are they trying to figure out how this whole wedding planning thing works? Then be the person to give them that advice! They will remember this when it comes time to make a purchase.

You can't propose marriage on the first date and expect to get a "yes," but you can propose something that is proportionate to the amount of trust that your potential client has in you.

I teach my clients to think about the first step they want people to take, and I suggest making that something small like asking them to provide their email in exchange for something like a helpful eBook, checklist or video. This way, you can start to build a relationship with them via email, and you're not just pouncing on them trying to get them to commit right now.

Take some time today to examine your website and figure out what you are asking people to do.

Are you trying to marry them or are you offering to take them on a first date?

The *know, like, trust factor* is incredibly important in marketing. People don't do business with people until they feel like they know, like and trust them.

What can you offer your potential clients to help them get to know, like and trust you *before* you ask them to call to book you?

Here's a tip to get your gears turning: answer their biggest questions.

If you're a wedding planner and the most common question you get is, "When do I need to book each of my vendors?" offer a timeline or a checklist in exchange for their email! You'll answer their question, build that crucial *know, like, trust* factor and be able to market to them via email. It's a win–win–win.

That's not all, though. There are other things

you can do with your website to build that *know, like, trust* factor.

Have you had styled shoots featured on blogs or in magazines? Showcase those logos proudly in an 'As Seen On' box on your site! Those logos provide social proof.

Social proof is a psychological phenomenon we all experience when we see that someone is trusted by others and you begin to trust them too. It's the positive version of guilt by association.

There have been studies that demonstrate the power of social proof including one from the Washington Post that showed that positive social proof was more influential than saving money.

This is why every McDonald's sign says "Billions and billions served." Knowing that billions of people have had something is reassuring to the part of us that likes to avoid risk. If you've ever made a decision based on an Amazon review by a total stranger, you've acted because of social proof. If you've ever been impressed that someone has been featured in a particular blog or magazine, that's social proof at work.

Displaying where you've been featured isn't the only way to build credibility through social proof. Your testimonials play a *huge* role in this, but not just any testimonial will do the trick. I see a lot of bland testimonials that say things like "She was great!" or "We're so happy we worked with you." That only gives you a tiny piece of the story. If you want your testimonials to help you make more sales, they have to describe the experience of the client before, during and after working with you. You have to tell their story, their full story.

Here is an example of a testimonial I have from a client that shows the before, during and after.

> "Before I joined The Wedding Business Collective, I was having such a hard time booking clients. I just could not understand why I was not getting the clients that I wanted/needed. I took all the proper steps to create the business, and now I was failing without even starting. I felt aggravated, mad, sad, and most of all depressed.

When Heidi reviewed my website, it took her all of 5 minutes to pinpoint the problem. I sounded too stuffy and corporate on my website, and I wasn't connecting with my ideal client.

Heidi gave me plenty of pointers and suggestions that I implemented by December 27th (that date was a personal business goal). On January 1st, I got my first inquiry, but I was too excited and also nervous, so I totally blew it. However, I was not discouraged because now I knew that my client was out there and soon they would be looking for me. And I was absolutely right!

Today makes exactly two months since I made the changes that Heidi suggested and I have booked four clients that have paid their retainer. I am waiting on another two tentative clients to pay their retainer and I have a proposal to send off!

If you are thinking of joining The Wedding Business Collective, I strongly urge you to do so. I actually came across The Wedding Business Collective in May or June 2016. I thought about it, but I did not join until December. Imagine where I could have been more than six months ago if I had joined when I originally saw The Wedding Business Collective! It's a good thing I eventually joined; it has been a tremendous blessing to my business! THANK YOU, HEIDI!!"

Amelia Washington
www.ameliasevents.com

This testimonial gives a much different feeling to the reader than something like "Heidi was great, and I loved working with her." You can identify with the 'feels' of the person before, during and after working with me. That is exactly the type of testimonial that will help you get more clients.

> **Download my exact email templates for getting testimonials like these at www.evolveyourweddingbusiness.com/book.**

Getting that first "yes"

Email marketing fills in the gap between "I'm just researching and I'm not ready to have a sales conversation yet" and "I'm ready to work with you, let's talk." That gap is *gigantic* (it can be several months long), and it's where decisions are made, so it's important that you insert yourself here.

Let's say someone finds you today, but they're not ready to book you for another 3, 6 or 12 months (and that's very possible considering that most couples spend hundreds of hours researching and planning their weddings). What are the chances of them remembering your site when they are ready to work with someone? Do you remember every website you went to today, much less six months ago? They might *love* you but simply just forget to come back to you, and that's a silly reason to miss out on a booking.

With email marketing, you allow them to sign up for your email list so that you can keep in touch with them. Couples don't make these decisions quickly, they spend hundreds of hours researching, so the chances of them booking you off of their first website visit are pretty slim. You could see this as an annoyance, or you could use it to your advantage.

How do you use it to your advantage? You create an opportunity for a first date by offering something of value in exchange for their email address. Offering something in exchange for the person joining your email list is incredibly effective, and this thing that you're offering is called an opt-in offer.

Here are some examples of opt-in offers:

- One member of *The Wedding Business Collective* created an invitation wording guide because as a stationer, she found that her potential clients were unsure about how their invitations were supposed to or could be worded. She solves that problem for them with her guide.

- Another *Wedding Business Collective* member created an eBook called *7 Smart Ways To Keep Your Sanity While Planning Your Wedding*. As a planner, she helps people stay on track with their planning without losing their mind.

- One of my former clients created a little black book of recommended vendors in the area because as a photographer, he was getting hired early on in the planning process and his couples were asking him for recommendations. That's perfect for a couple in the research phase!

Go back to your interview responses. What did people tell you they found frustrating, hesitated about or wish they would have known? These are perfect topics for your first date opt-in offer.

We already covered how your blog can bring people to your site, but you can also use it to promote your opt-in offer. If your first date email opt-in offer is a checklist for planning your wedding, it will make sense to promote that within a blog post about the planning mistakes that couples make and how to avoid them.

GOING STEADY

Your potential client downloaded your opt-in offer and enjoyed that first date. They're digging you, and now you're going steady (and yes, I'm well aware I sound like I'm from the 1950s, but there isn't another term quite like it).

Now, how do you get from the first date to getting engaged?

You go on more dates via email marketing.

Your dates will consist of 2 types of emails: your autoresponder emails and your regular emails.

Your autoresponder is a series of emails that get sent to subscribers automatically (woohoo!) in the order you designate. You set it up once, and it works for you forever. It's freaking incredible! Every new subscriber goes through this series of emails upon signing up so I'm sure you can imagine that it's a pretty powerful selling tool.

Your autoresponder warms people up to you, positions you as the expert and presents your product or service as the clear solution to their problem. Instead of them going to your website and never coming back, they go to your website, sign up to your email list and get this autoresponder email series that takes them step by step through smashing their objections, teaching them about the value you provide and positioning you as the best choice for them.

Oh, and it does this all on autopilot. I can't emphasize that enough. Your email marketing efforts are doing a large part of the selling for you—automatically. How beautiful is that?

Not sure what to include in your autoresponder?

In *The Wedding Business Collective*, there is a full seven email series that I've written for you to take and tweak to fit you and use as your autoresponder. No more excuses, it's done for you. Easy peasy!

Visit www.theweddingbusinesscollective.com/booktrial to sign up for your free trial and start putting your email marketing machine together!

The other emails you'll send are your regular emails or broadcasts line up with your content schedule. If you're blogging each week, you send an email to your list each week to deliver that new post to them along with any promotional information or calls to action to get them to take the next step and book you.

If you think you just need more traffic...

It's true that only a certain percentage of your website visitors turn into clients. You could just send more people to your site to have the vast majority of them leave and never take action, or you can increase the percentage of people who turn into clients by allowing them to take a small first step (opting into your email list). Once you have your sales funnel in place, a larger percentage of people who visit your site will join your email list, and through the wonders of email marketing, more of them will become clients.

So yes, more traffic can help, but sending more traffic to a website that isn't set up to generate leads is like trying to fill a leaky bucket. Plug the hole in the bucket first by setting up your email marketing, then fill it.

So, what is the point of email marketing?

Having a website is par for the course, but are you using email marketing to turn your website into a lead generator? It is your website's job after all. Are you using an autoresponder to nurture those leads without having to do that work over and over again?

What's the point of email marketing? It makes generating leads and making sales easier, and who doesn't want that?

You don't have to rely on someone remembering to come back to your website when they're ready to buy. You can develop a relationship with them while they're in research mode and that has a HUGE impact on sales because when it's time for them to buy, guess who they're going to turn to? The wedding pro who has been helping them all along.

POPPING THE QUESTION

You and your potential client have been dating for a little while now. They know, like and trust you and they love your blog posts and emails.

They're getting closer to being ready to work with someone, so it only makes sense to pop the question at this point. The only difference between doing this in a relationship and in a business is that in a business you'll want to do pop the question more than once and in different ways.

Why? It's easy to think that you'll be the obvious choice but let's be honest, life is full of distractions. If you aren't reminding people how they can work with you, they will forget. The good news is there are many different ways of proposing to your potential client.

What getting engaged means is going to be different for each business, but it's the decision to make this relationship more serious before making a commitment to work with you. For many service-based businesses, getting engaged may be booking a consultation with you. Start by identifying what the 'getting engaged' action is for your potential clients.

Your potential client may be on the fence, and

we want them to make a decision, one way or another, about working with you. A great way to do that is to use your blog and email content to seal the deal.

Promotional content

A promotional email doesn't have to be the sort of thing that makes you squirm and feel gross as you're writing it. In fact, if it does, take a different approach. Instead of being the "BUY IT NOW!" infomercial salesperson, you can focus your promotional emails on a natural deadline (like their wedding date), the experience of working with you or a promotional offer.

If you were planning a wedding and you were coming up to the point where you needed to have your stationery ordered, wouldn't you like someone to inform you of that? A stationer could write a promotional blog post or email about how if you're getting married in December you need to order your stationery in the next month. Lay out the timelines they may not have considered like time to design, print, mail and get RSVPs and then tell them to click to schedule a consultation with you.

Urgency is an incredibly important component of getting someone off the fence and into action. After all, if there's no urgency, they'll just think "I'll do that later" and then never do it. It's in your potential client's best interest, and yours, to create genuine urgency. This is why sales always have a specific end date.

There is a difference between genuine and fake urgency. Genuine urgency is when you only have a few more spots left for clients, and you want to let your potential clients know that. Fake urgency is when you don't truly have a limited supply, but you say you do anyway to get people to take action. Urgency is a powerful motivator, and it's important to use it responsibly.

If you decide to do a short-term promotion, keep in mind that it doesn't have to be a traditional sale where you slash your prices, instead, you can add value to what the client is getting. An example of this is if your client books wedding photography by a certain date they'll receive a free engagement session that normally costs $500. You could also do a contest, a giveaway, a joint promotion with another wedding professional, your imagination is the limit. Just be sure that you use urgency to motivate clients to take you up on your offer.

Another way to promote your products and services is to tell the story of a client in the form of a case study. A lot of wedding professionals will showcase a recent wedding on their blog, but they don't make full use of that opportunity. Sure, it's great to show off photos of a recent wedding or a set of invitations you created, but when you turn that into a case study, it becomes a much more powerful way to move the reader to book that consultation with you.

Inside *The Wedding Business Collective*, I provide members with a done-for-you seven email autoresponder that contains a case study email. I wrote this email based on a testimonial one member had on her site:

Subject: He was blown away

Cann was blown away when he saw his wedding invitation suite that he didn't even think he was going to be able to afford.

When Cann came to me, he made it clear that it was VERY important to him and his partner that they have invitations that were unique, personalized, and made with a certain level of care that a big box company would skimp on. He loved foil-stamped invitations but didn't think he was going to be able to afford them. You should have seen his face when I presented him with an option he could afford. He was thrilled because the foil gave his invitations the glamour that he and his partner wanted them to have so badly.

Like many of my clients, Cann had lots of questions because he never had done this before, but I made sure not only to answer all of them but to give him advice that helped him.

Cann was surprised that I loved his idea for his wedding programs. He thought I wouldn't like it because they didn't match the invitations. Like I said in my email about wedding stationery being boring, there isn't just one way to do things and I LOVE that about the creative people I get to work with.

Here's what Cann had to say about what I did with his idea for his wedding programs:

"She made my idea even better. That's what Ashleigh does; she can make your stationery ideas come to life exactly as you wanted it or she can enhance it!"

Ready to see the final product for yourself?

<photo of Cann's stationery>

If you're like Cann and you want invitations that are unique, personalized, and made with a certain level of care that a big box company would skimp on, click here to schedule a free call with me!

I can't wait to hear all about your ideas!

Ashleigh

This email works because you're painting a picture of what it's like to work with you from initial contact through to the finished product. Doing so takes the risk and uncertainty away and makes working with you more appealing. It's also not about you, and that makes it come across very differently than if you emailed someone telling them how great you are and why they should work with you. Instead, your actual previous client has done that for you.

Regular ongoing promotion

There are many different ways to do regular promotion in small but meaningful ways. When you send out a broadcast email about your latest blog post, include a call to action that gives people an option to say yes to you. Just like proposing to a person, you can't get a yes unless you ask.

A simple way to do this is to add something to your email, even as a P.S., with something like "Ready to get started planning your wedding together? Click here to schedule your consultation so we can see if we're a good fit for one another."

Michele Botnick is a romance travel specialist

and a member of *The Wedding Business Collective*, and she's making email marketing work for her. She took the autoresponder available to all members of *The Wedding Business Collective* and added in some wedding date specific emails (because it's natural urgency), and they are working extremely well for her. When she started the wedding date specific emails, she had generated three honeymoon inquiries from them within just three days!

It's important that in any communication where you want people to take a specific action like buying something or booking a consultation that you give them a specific call to action telling them what to do and how to do it. Michele told people to click to book a free, no obligation 1-hour consultation with her. It can be that simple!

9

Measure What Matters

Marketing is an ongoing experiment, and if you don't track the results, you'll never know what works and what doesn't. That means you won't know what to do more of and what to do less of.

Back in my days as an employee, I worked as the marketing manager at a company that did a lot of things in weird ways. They had no control over their website and no way to make any changes to it. It was a mess. One day in a meeting I found out that mailers were going out and when I asked about them they said they spent $500-$1,000 each month sending out direct mail to people they thought might be interested in working with them.

Since this was news to me, I said: "Oh, okay cool, how is that working for you?"

::crickets::

They just stared at me. They were spending $500-$1,000 per month on something that they weren't measuring. They had no idea if this was working for them and if it was worth the expense because they never bothered to measure the results.

I wish I could tell you that they're an outlier, but a lot of businesses market without measuring the results. Why? Because it feels good to throw money at something and count that as getting closer to your goal. It's the same mentality as signing up for a gym membership and never using it. You feel like you did something, but really you didn't do anything. At least not anything that you can prove.

You'll never know if you're on track with your goals unless you stop and measure. After all, what gets measured gets improved. That's why I'm such a big fan of setting up CEO dates.

CEO dates are regular meetings with yourself where you go over the key metrics for your business & goals. This might be the number of people who scheduled a consult, number of booked clients, email subscribers, revenue, etc.

If you don't set aside time on a regular basis (I recommend doing this weekly), you'll never know if you're moving forward or backward. You might feel like you're moving forward but check with the numbers, they never lie.

So what should you track?

There are some things that all businesses should track such as revenue and the number of inquiries received any given month and how many became clients. Most of the things that you should track depend on your business and your goals, but they can be broken down into leading metrics and lagging metrics.

Leading metrics are the things that lead to a particular outcome whereas lagging metrics are the results. An example of a lagging metrics is sales because that is the result. The leading metrics that lead to that result can be things like consultations, inquiries or email subscribers. If you know that you book one client for every two consultations you have, it then becomes easier to focus on taking action to get the number of consultations you need to generate the number of sales you need.

Beyond the numbers

Numbers aren't the only things you should measure in your business. Every week in my CEO date I ask myself three very important questions:

1. What went well this week?
2. What could have gone better?
3. What will I do to improve that next week?

These questions are important to ask yourself so that you can take control of the situation and steer yourself into having more successful weeks. It also forces you to stop for a moment and take stock of your accomplishments. It's far too easy as an entrepreneur to steamroll over your accomplishments because you're so focused on what's next and this exercise helps you realize how much progress you're really making.

10

Test & Tweak

Failure is not a bad thing. Yup, that's right. Failure is not bad; it's how we learn things. If you never continued after falling, you wouldn't know how to walk. You have to try things, fall on your ass, and then learn from that.

If you try something and it doesn't work, that's fine. We're all in the business of experimentation so don't set yourself up to think it's as binary as success or failure because it's not. It's a test, everything is, and you tweak it and move on with what you've learned. When something doesn't work, that is very important because it's giving you data and feedback and you can take that and figure out what to change . . . Or you can collapse into a ball of sorrow and self-loathing. That is your choice. You decide how you view things like failure and how you react to it, no one else.

We're all scientists here, and business is a huge series of experiments. The outcome isn't tied to you or your worth; it's just an experiment. If scientists looked at experiments that way, they would have quit when the first thing they tried didn't cure every disease. That mindset shift is crucial in business.

Instead of beating yourself up when something doesn't go the way you thought it would, think like a scientist. Why didn't it go the way you thought? What could you change in order to change the outcome? What could you test next time? There is a lot of value in failed experiments if you use them to figure out how to get it right the next time.

If you find that you're getting all of your results from a few things you're doing, you can focus on those. You don't have to treat every marketing tactic equally when they're not delivering equal results. Just don't cut them off prematurely. You can always tweak them to get better results.

If you see that a few of your blog posts are much more popular than others, dig into that. What do you think is drawing people to them? How could you do more of it to create more successful posts?

If you see that some of your social media posts are performing better than others, ask yourself why. Is it that they're all worded a certain way? Are they all focused on a similar topic? Do they all contain images?

Tyese Knight, a wedding planner and member of *The Wedding Business Collective*, has gone from Facebook ads that were generating traffic but not many email sign-ups to Facebook ads that generate both traffic and email sign-ups by adopting a testing & tweaking mindset. She could have thrown in the towel after things didn't go great with her first ad, but instead, she asked for help on how she could improve the page she was sending people to generate more email sign-ups. We decided on some improvements she could make and combined with her decision to use the images that generated the most clicks in the first ad campaign, it has created a Facebook ad campaign that is generating leads for her.

If at first you don't succeed, that's okay! Dig into why that is and what you can change to improve your results.

11

So Where Do You Go from Here?

Congratulations! You've made it through a process to find the marketing plan that will work for your specific business. This is the hard, behind-the-scenes work that isn't sexy but is essential, and because you're one of the wedding professionals who has done this work, you're going to see more success as a result.

You now have the coveted blueprint that is going to guide you to success in your wedding business. No more guessing what you should or shouldn't be doing to attract your ideal client. Woohoo! I'm doing a happy dance for you!

However, your work is not done.

You know how to speak to your ideal client, where to reach them, how to attract them and the marketing tactics to use for each part of the sales funnel, but when it comes to the nitty-gritty details of how to do each of these marketing tactics you may need some more help.

That's why I created *The Wedding Business Collective*, to provide you with all of the training, support, accountability, knowledge and feedback that will make your wedding business a success as you move forward.

When you're a member of *The Wedding Business Collective*, you get access to . . .

- A comprehensive library of marketing and business training worth over $3,000 that covers everything from selling with email marketing, attracting your ideal clients, blogging, Facebook ads, SEO, pricing, productivity and more and it is always growing to accommodate the needs of the members.

- My ongoing personal support.

- A live monthly mastermind call where you can ask any and all of your questions.

- Access to quick wins trainings where you'll get bite-sized training in 10 minute chunks that you can take action on right away.

- Access to our private community of wedding professionals just like you to collaborate with, learn from, support & get support from. They'll also help keep you accountable and give you feedback when you need it and be real with you.

- A video critique of a member's site each month (and you can submit your site too!).

- Accountability partner program so you have someone to help make sure you get things done.

- VIP access to everything that is added to The Collective in the future.

If you're serious about building a successful wedding business, then *The Wedding Business Collective* is a no-brainer; and to make it even easier for you to get the knowledge, support and resources you need, we're offering a FREE 10-Day Trial so that you can take it for a test drive.

And in the very unlikely chance that you don't find it useful, no worries! You can cancel with just a few clicks.

Start your FREE 10-Day Trial at www.theweddingbusinesscollective.com/ booktrial

Whether you want to be like Esme Krahn who is now reaching her ideal clients and they're willing to pay what she's worth . . .

Or like Ashleigh Pritchard who had her most productive year ever and booked her most profitable client ever . . .

Or like Marie Burns Holzer who went from unhappily working with just anyone to working with her ideal clients who are more profitable and make her happier in her work . . .

Or like Amelia Washington went from 0 clients and 0 inquiries to 4 booked clients and 3 more tentative clients in under 2 months. . .

The Wedding Business Collective can help you do that. **Start your FREE 10-Day Trial at www.theweddingbusinesscollective.com/ booktrial**

Acknowledgements

Thank you to all of the Launch Team members and wedding industry friends & colleagues who helped with the launch of this book and supported me along the way. I love and appreciate each and every one of you!

Amanda Shuman

Andrew Hellmich

Annette Stepanian

Arius Jacks

Ashley Miller Robinson

Bob Graham

Brenda Cadman

Chamira Young

Christie Osborne

Daniel Waters

Debbie Orwat

Desiree Brooks

Eddie Babbage

Esme Krahn

Gina Amos

Kellie Daab

Kylie Carlson

Jaimie Burke

Jared Bauman

Jennifer Murray

Josh Withers

Julie Klima Casey

Karina Brown

Katherine Healy Brown

Katie Frost

Katie Hamuka

Kayla Pickrell

Keneshia Raymond

Kimberli Lowe

Kimberly Lehman

Lindsey Cowen

Lindsey Nickel

Maigen Thomas

Marie Burns Holzer

Pri Kruijen

Roger Knight

Rosa Clark

Sabrina Cadini

Shana Shears

Shannon DePalma

Shawn Broussard

Stacey Kerslake

Susan Obregon

Tejal Patel

The fabulous team at Honeybook & The Rising
Tide Society

About the Author

Heidi Thompson is the founder of Evolve Your Wedding Business where she specializes in business and marketing strategy for wedding professionals. She helps wedding professionals around the world grow their businesses and reach their goals without going crazy in the process. Her business & marketing expertise has been featured on several wedding and business outlets including The Huffington Post, Social Media Examiner, Wedding Business Magazine, Sprouting Photographer, Photo Biz Xposed & she's an advisory board member for the UK Academy Of Wedding & Event Planning.

Printed in Great Britain
by Amazon